no problem

"Gentle, wise, and sensible advice from an experienced spiritual guide to help you find God in all that you do, and in all that you are—and will be."

James Martin, S.J.
Author of *The Jesuit Guide to (Almost) Everything*

"In this thin but rich book, seasoned psychologist and spiritual guide Robert Wicks takes us on a healing walk through the spiritual malaise of much of modern life. *No Problem* is filled with fresh insights to help us around and over the gritty road bumps of everyday life. This is spiritual writing at its best—firmly grounded in the wisdom figures of the past and present and psychologically informed with the best of holistic thinking."

Donald Cozzens
Author of *Notes from the Underground*

"From the opening lines of *No Problem*, Robert Wicks identified what seems to be my eternal struggle: allowing my faith to become more than the words I profess and pray, allowing it to infuse my life with the joy and hope that is at its core. I found myself not wanting to move through the book too quickly, but savoring the daily reflections the way they were meant to be read. This book is perfect for anyone who tries daily to live the faith in the fullest sense but too often gets caught up in the chaos of life around us."

Mary DeTurris Poust
Author of *Cravings*

RELATED BOOKS BY ROBERT J. WICKS

Streams of Contentment: Lessons I Learned on My Uncle's Farm

Prayerfulness: Awakening to the Fullness of Life

Everyday Simplicity: A Practical Guide to Spiritual Growth

Crossing the Desert: Learning to Let Go, See Clearly, and Live Simply

Riding the Dragon: 10 Lessons for Inner Strength in Challenging Times

Simple Changes: Quietly Overcoming Barriers to Personal and Professional Growth

Seeds of Sensitivity: Deepening Your Spiritual Life

Snow Falling on Snow: Themes from the Spiritual Landscape of Robert J. Wicks

Bounce: Living the Resilient Life

ROBERT J. WICKS

no problem

turning the

next corner

in your

spiritual life

SORIN BOOKS Notre Dame, Indiana

www.sorinbooks.com

Paperback ISBN-13 978-1-933495-64-4

E-book ISBN-13 978-1-933495-65-1

Cover image © Thinkstock.

Cover and text design by Brian C. Conley.

Printed and bound in the United States of America.

Library of Congress Cataloging-in-Publication Data
Wicks, Robert J.
 No problem : turning the next corner in your spiritual life / Robert J. Wicks.
    pages cm
 Includes bibliographical references.
 ISBN 1-933495-64-2 (978-1-933495-64-4)
 1. Spiritual life--Catholic Church. 2. Spiritual formation--Catholic Church. I. Title.
 BX2350.3.W53 2014
 248.4'82--dc23
                              2013044718

*For the Carmelite Sisters of Baltimore.
Thank you for modeling for me what it means
to be simultaneously contemplative, relational,
and relevant in a challenging world.*

"Life is not a problem to be solved
but a mystery to be lived."

—Gabriel Marcel

Contents

Part II: The Call and Three Doorways

Part III: Developing Your Own Inner Workshop of Virtue

A Brief Introduction:
Create an Inner Workshop

Peter France, the former host of the popular BBC radio program *The Living World*, relates in his book *Patmos* that this Greek isle has long had a remarkable healing impact on people. He notes:

> It changes people. . . . In the age of myth, Patmos was a place where the veil that separated the everyday from the eternal was thin. Some feel it remains so [today]. . . . [Spiritual father] Christodoulos traveled to Constantinople to ask the emperor for permission to create what he called "a workshop of virtue" on the island. . . . There was a sense of the numinous here, a presence even I felt as a prompting to awe.

The question this book will ask is the following: What if such a "workshop" could be created or strengthened within us so we could move forward in the spiritual life with the tools we need when we face the challenges of the unknown future? However, for this to be possible, we must be willing to do inner work with discipline, complete honesty, and openness. As spiritual mentor and psychologist Jack Kornfield notes in his enchanting book, *After the Ecstasy, the Laundry*, "to sustain a spiritual practice demands our steady attention. The first task, then, in almost any spiritual voyage, is to quiet ourselves enough to listen to the voices of our hearts, to listen to that which is beyond our daily affairs . . . [to] step out of our usual roles . . . [and] to become receptive and open."

Crossing new spiritual thresholds in life takes great faith. It is a little like walking down a familiar street and being aware that we must eventually turn the corner and not know what we will find there. But what we need most is not simply knowledge, as important as that is. While passion is also required, that too is not enough. Beyond these, the development of an inner workshop calls us to a *radical change in attitude*. This change in attitude is expressed well by the twentieth-century French philosopher Gabriel Marcel, who said, "Life is not a problem to be solved, but a mystery to be lived." How often do we hear from our coworkers, our family and friends, and even in restaurants and stores the phrase, "No problem!" What if we were to start thinking about our spiritual lives in this way? Imagine the inner space that this might create, allowing us to see our inner lives as blessed gifts to be fully enjoyed and freely shared with others. That would be, indeed, a radical change in attitude.

Yet, such an attitude of intense freedom and openness is like the shy stag of a mystical forest: it is elusive and cannot be sought directly, although when it is present it is easily recognized and felt. We can feel it in the presence of persons who seem to embody such virtues or traits as gratitude, natural compassion, humility, and a deep appreciation of the necessity of healthy interest in *both* self and others as a way of being open to God. This is what inner formation and what this book, for that matter, is about.

Why I Wrote This Book Now

Recently, I decided to move away from my full-time teaching position at Loyola University Maryland. My goal was to open up more free space to write and give presentations on resilience, maintaining a healthy perspective, and the integration of psychology and spirituality. This turning of the *next* corner in my life had, and I suspect will continue to have, many foreseen and unforeseen consequences. Past approaches may not be sufficient. New ones will need to be created or gracefully greeted. A lot remains unknown, and the mystery of life, as I view the brief time ahead, is surely precious. As I quietly reflected on this reality, I realized again—this time with a seemingly greater sensitivity because of my own situation—how important inner formation is throughout all of our lives.

As other writers on the inner life would remind us, there is no spiritual retirement. Our healthy psychological attitude and spiritual outlook are the elements that can turn sadness into new learning and greater inner depth. On the other hand, a negative psychological attitude and spiritual outlook can result in our missing so many of the beautiful ordinary joys before us. And so in the preparation of this book I wanted to revisit some of the simple, but essential, lessons of inner formation. I made this inner workshop for myself and wanted to also share it with others who may be turning the next corner in their own spiritual life.

The Approach Taken

The chapters are quite brief, and the approach suggested is quite straightforward. Simply read a chapter either in the morning or evening, and seek to take to heart the story and point made over the next twenty-four hours. Don't analyze it. Don't ask yourself whether or not you were already aware of the point being made; as a matter of fact, I would be surprised if you weren't. Formation isn't about the new; it is more about how we can *renew*, come home to ourselves . . . and God.

"Simply" carry the themes and stories provided within you for a while during the day and reflect back on them for a few seconds as you go about your daily activities. Remember as well to recall them before you fall asleep. This will give the themes, drawn from both the saints and sages of the past and current spiritual guides, an opportunity to be seeded and ripen. In other words, in your busy day give yourself some room to reflect and breathe. In this way you will be inviting God to come to occupy the space within you. That's what an inner "workshop of virtue" requires.

And so each theme presented is an invitation to enhance the spirit of receptiveness and openness to an alternative, richer path than that which the world can offer. In the process of developing an inner "workshop of virtue," we can change, and our compassion toward others can deepen as well. Why is this so? Our lives become centered on God. When this occurs, we know it, for we feel greater freedom, peace, love, and clarity. Where does a person begin such a profound process? *Just start where you are.*

Following these twenty chapters of reflections, a brief section is presented on Jesus' central call and the three doorways we must continually walk through in the spiritual life. The purpose of this section is to demonstrate where the twenty lessons are meant to lead us.

Finally, the last section, a month's worth of simple questions and exercises, provides a way to truly actualize one's own unique "workshop of virtue." It allows the reader to personalize and fulfill in a profound way the one thing necessary for the spiritual life, which until now may have been—at least partially—missing: living in Christ with depth, peace, meaning, and compassion. In time, the process may offer us the chance to turn over a new leaf and live more transparently, simply, and joyously so others can, in turn, benefit from the journey with us *now* . . . the journey we have possibly only wished for up to this point.

Before delving further into the main three parts of this book, each of us should ask ourselves this question: How much do I really want to do the work that this inner workshop requires? There is no partial spirituality or spiritual retirement once we have committed ourselves. Personal inner formation is not about adding a few things to Sunday Mass. It is about being open, in St. Paul's words, to putting on the new self, to *change*. It is not about simply deepening your prayer life, although that is certainly a significant part of it. It is about changing the total character of the way you live, see yourself, reach out to others, and let go.

Spiritual formation is undertaken so we don't waste our time in life. This book is about offering ways to soften our soul so the truth and fullness of what God promised is welcomed more completely.

The messages are simple. The possibilities, with God's grace, are profound. The openness and commitment needed are complete. Yet, if the desire is there, then God is already alongside us. You don't need to put on any special clothing or be at a certain level of interior maturity. Just take each step as it comes. *Just start where you are.*

Part I

Twenty Lessons in Personal Inner Formation

I.

Live (Don't Only Say) a Simple Prayer

One of the great joys in my life has been the opportunity to meet so many dedicated, talented, and compassionate people in my mentoring and therapy work. Among them was a very committed Christian who demonstrated her love for God and others through acts of charity, attendance at daily Mass, and faithfulness to her prayer life. Despite all of this good work and spiritual discipline, she was a gold-medal worrier. This was not only a problem for her, but it weighed heavily on her family as well. Negativity is very contagious. When someone who is troubled enters the room, you can immediately feel the spirits of those present lower a bit. When that person is someone you live with (or possibly you!), it is even worse.

In response to the heaviness both the woman and her family were feeling, my first goal was aimed at helping her to recognize and then challenge her dysfunctional cognitions (ways of thinking, perceiving, and understanding). To some extent, this psychological process lessened the amount of negativity she was carrying and inadvertently sharing with her family. However, it became obvious to me that her situation needed to be addressed on a deeper spiritual level as well.

And so the next time she came in for a session, I said to her, "You seem to be such a very prayerful Catholic. Yet, you seem to neglect the one prayer acknowledging a simple call from God that is at the heart of the spiritual life." As I anticipated, she looked surprised and asked eagerly (because she was very open to deepening her inner life), "What prayer are you talking about?"

"Well," I responded, "maybe it is best demonstrated through a brief story. If you gave a little girl a present at Christmas or for her birthday, what would be the best way for her to thank you? Expressing her gratitude in words would be nice. However, how much richer her statement of gratitude would be if you saw her fully enjoying the gift and freely sharing it with her friends and siblings. The same can be said about the gift of life we have been given by God and our grateful response. Sure, we could say our thanks in words, and as the psalmists suggest we should do that. But how much more real and compelling our prayer of thanks would be if we could totally enjoy the gift of life God has bestowed on us and share it naturally with others without expecting anything (not a smile, a word of thanks, or their following a suggestion we might offer them) in return."

The example of the child and the gift must have struck a chord in the woman. She seemed to be awakened to looking at her life differently and ready to act on this insight in ways that would make her life a little lighter and her compassion a bit more joyous.

The call to live in peace and joy and to share it with others is quite simple. Yet, for most of us at different turns in the day, week, month, year, or our lives in general, it is still not easy. Self-compassion and compassion for others go hand in hand. Just as Jesus calls us to see others as being made in the image and likeness of God (what is referred to as *"imago Dei"*), we must simultaneously remember the same about ourselves. When people can see that we are giving not out of duty, guilt, or fear that someone will think less of us, the gift they receive from us will be greater. The reason is that it is being given naturally out of our own sense of being gifted. And, in gratitude to God, we are enjoying these very gifts to the full rather than ignoring them.

Scripture scholar Walter Bruggemann called such an underappreciation of the graces around us "under-living." To live in such a manner is so foolish, given how short life is. Also, "under-living" doesn't set the stage for increasing our compassion toward others. Instead, it simply limits our ability in the long run to share ourselves with others. Foolish, isn't it?

Robert Ellsberg, in his insight-filled book *The Saints' Guide to Happiness*, pointed this out with respect to Dorothy Day, who many consider a modern-day saint because of her steadfast commitment to the poor. Ellsberg writes:

> Keenly attuned to the suffering of others, [Dorothy Day] remained equally sensitive to the signs of beauty and ever mindful of what she called "the duty of delight." She read the news in the light of eternity. And she had the remarkable effect, when you were with her, of making you feel that you could change the world, and be a better person, and that such an understanding would be an enormous adventure. . . . No one who ever observed how she savored a cup of instant coffee or the rare luxury of a fresh roll, how she enjoyed watching the shifting tides of Raritan Bay off Staten Island or listened raptly to the Saturday afternoon opera broadcasts on the radio, could fail to detect the quality that Teilhard de Chardin described as a "zest for living."

Jesus, in John 10:10, said, "I have come to bring you fullness." The simple question for us is: How are we embracing that fullness in gratitude and freely sharing it with others? How we live in response to this simple, powerful question is at the heart of the spiritual life and our personal inner formation.

2.

Rediscover the Lost Virtue of the Desert

My daughter, son-in-law, and two grandchildren were sitting around the kitchen table for dinner. Once the meal was done, my daughter looked at her children and asked, "What are you particularly good at doing? In other words, what gifts do you think God has given to you so you can help others?"

My granddaughters love these types of questions and launched into sharing a pretty full list of what modern positive psychology would call "signature strengths." After hearing this recitation by both of them, my son-in-law asked, "Well, what about humility? Neither of you mentioned that." To which my youngest granddaughter, Emily, immediately asked, "What's humility?"

My son-in-law is not so young that the Internet is his only source of information, so he said in reply, "Well, get the dictionary, and let's look it up."

In response, the youngest scurried to find the dictionary, grabbed hold of it, and handed it to her dad. He found the entry for "humility," read the definition out loud, and then asked, "Well, what person comes to mind when you hear this description?" Both of them and their mother immediately responded with great enthusiasm, "Mom-Mom!" referring to my wife. My son-in-law then asked, "Well, what about Pop-Pop?" to which they all shook their heads from side to side and said, "No, not Pop-Pop!"

No matter how much we may value the spiritual life, the virtue of humility is an elusive one—especially for Pop-Pop! Yet we must all seek it every day because it is the very "soil" in which personal spiritual formation grows. Without humility, response to God's call is nearly impossible. Without it we will not be able to take our place in the world while not being *of* the world. Yet, despite this reality, humility is in short supply today.

As we look around the world—and even the Church—we rarely see the face of humility. That is one of the reasons why I suspect that the choice of Pope Francis was such a particular cause for joy among so many Catholics, whether they called themselves conservative, middle-of-the-road, or liberal. True ordinariness is tangible holiness, and we experience this holiness for ourselves when we encounter the spirit of humility in another person or, without labeling it as such, in ourselves.

The reason that humility is also at the heart of the spiritual journey is as follows:

When you take knowledge and you add humility, you get wisdom. And when you add that wisdom to compassion, you get love, and God is love.

Knowing this, though, is only part of the challenge since humility cannot be sought directly. To do so would paradoxically be an act of pride and egoism. Humility is a grace freely given to us by God. However, this doesn't mean we should do nothing to enhance the soil in which humility can grow. For instance, here are some of the ways we can welcome and respect this gift:

- Recognize times when we compare ourselves favorably—or unfavorably, for that matter—with others; when we don't over- or underestimate ourselves, life is much more pleasant. A fruit of humility is the ability to recognize *both* our gifts and our growing edges with a sense of equanimity.
- Appreciate how much others have played in our successes—no matter how hard we also may have worked; no achievement is obtained by one person in a vacuum.

- Notice when we draw attention to ourselves and our accomplishments and possessions, not as a celebration of gratitude for the blessings received, but as a sign of our own superiority.
- Avoid, or catch ourselves when we are tempted to use, sarcasm or humor at the expense of others.

These are but a number of simple steps to keep us aware of the need to see ourselves and our lives totally, clearly, and gratefully. Humility is certainly the spiritual ingredient that makes life so much more tasty and easy to live without a sense of distress. It is also tied to the psychological ability to have sound self-esteem because it helps us avoid the dangers and distortion of overconfidence on the one hand and inordinate self-doubt on the other. Humility clears the lens in which we view ourselves and allows us to enjoy the gifts we have been given and to share them freely, not being concerned about their limits. Instead, we do what we can, enjoy what we have been given, and let God take care of the rest.

3.

Look Outward Too

The central goal of inner formation is sometimes overlooked: to be open to "the other" in a richer, freer way. When we forget this, we can easily make errors. The giveaway is when one becomes moody and inappropriately self-centered. Meditation and contemplation are times to be open to God, not simply focused on our own views and needs—as important as it is for us to be aware of and tend to them. Even when self-examination and attention to major events in our own lives have led to good insights and consequent actions, God will still call us beyond a healthy interest in ourselves to see things in new, possibly greater ways. I learned this in a way that impacted me quite deeply.

One Sunday, the Jesuit priest presiding at Mass shared with the congregation that he had lost his mother when he was very young. She hadn't died suddenly, so there were many thoughts, feelings, and experiences that he recalled during her final days and for years afterward. He hadn't shied away from them when they came up in prayer, because he wanted to grasp the events and his responses to them fully. Although painful at times, this honesty and openness proved fruitful for him and for those to whom he ministered who had lost someone close to them—especially when it happened to them at an early age when they were most vulnerable.

However, at one point he shared that he was graced with a different question during a period of prayerful silence and solitude. Instead of looking at how he felt about this loss, he asked himself, "How did my mother feel since she knew she was dying and would leave both me and my father?"

Prior to this, he had appropriately focused on his own sense of hurt and loss, as he most assuredly should have. Now he was being called to think of the other and her sense of what was about to happen. Today, readiness to think of the other and willingness to respond can be seen in those who interact with this priest. His spiritual maturity has allowed him to tend to what is necessary in himself while not getting overly involved in himself. Thus he can be open to the needs, lessons, and call of God that can only come to us through interaction with, and concern for, others.

Here are some questions we can ask ourselves as we search for a similar spiritual maturity:

- When people speak about their own painful experiences, do we turn the conversation back to the suffering or negative events that have happened to us?
- As we appropriately hold in one hand our own hurtful memories and the negative events of life without denying, minimizing, or avoiding them, are we also able to hold in the other hand an appreciation of other people's crosses and to be open to where such past or current sadness might lead us spiritually?
- How has our compassion for others become richer because of difficult experiences and awareness of the pain in our own lives?
- How have our losses and trauma freed us from being inordinately focused on what is unimportant?
- In what ways has a deep understanding of the pain of others who are close to us, and even those with whom we have had no personal contact, helped us to be more grateful for all we have had and still have in life?

The more we can question ourselves in a gentle, constant way about the pain in ourselves and others, the more complete the picture we will be able to obtain of what God is seeking to teach us amid our suffering. When we move too quickly to solve, eliminate, or get beyond our own unhappy experiences, we run the risk of missing the signposts God has put there for us to understand both our lives and those of others in the world. Once again, a major gift of spiritual wisdom is seeing more of the *total* picture, not just what appears to be the case in our own particular life.

4.

Appreciate the Strength of Inner Simplicity

Amid myriad activities and multidirectional pulls in the course of a day and throughout our lives, most of us have a natural yearning for simplicity. Personal spiritual formation is also centered on honoring the simple life. However, simplicity is usually not quite what we imagine or what our culture says it is.

Secular books on simplicity focus on downsizing through the elimination of activities and dropping of unnecessary things. Although this may be one of the results of reviewing our cluttered lives, spiritual simplicity focuses on something more. It seeks to prune our inner attitude toward life and create a disposition to embrace what is truly essential in the eyes of God. True simplicity, and the freedom that is one of its major fruits, results when God's will (theonomy) and our will (autonomy) intersect.

Monk and scientist Matthieu Ricard in his extraordinary book *Happiness* writes, "Simplifying one's life to extract its quintessence is the most rewarding of all pursuits. . . . It doesn't mean giving up what is truly beneficial, but finding out what really matters."

Once, during a brief lecture tour of Thailand and Japan, I sat in a little office in Bangkok with a Maryknoll Missioner priest who directed a program in Thailand for refugees from neighboring war-torn lands. The refugees were often treated brutally by the regime in power. Some were finally able to escape, but the trauma they experienced often left deep scars that needed time to heal. In some cases, a full healing was impossible, since permanent psychological and physical damage had been done.

As I was sitting with the priest, I was distracted by a face with a wide-eyed look that appeared in a little window that led to the community room down the hall. As quickly as the face appeared, it suddenly disappeared. Puzzled, I looked at the priest. He smiled and said, "He is one of our residents. In Thailand, when they refer to such a person, they point to their own heads and say, 'Not full!'"

The priest went on to say, "When he first came here, I was overwhelmed by all the difficulties he was experiencing. So I said to the staff, who seemed perfectly fine with his staying with us, 'This man is so troubled. What can we possibly do for him?' To this, they all looked puzzled, and finally one of them said to me, 'Why, love him of course,' which made me just beam. Their solution came from the simplicity spawned by a spiritual heart that taught me I needed to look at how I can lose my way at times."

Personal spiritual formation is about only one thing: *love*. This love extends to God, others, and ourselves simultaneously. If this is not seen as true, the whole process of formation can degrade into a search for the right techniques or laws. One theologian once proclaimed that Christ didn't call us to a new religion, but to life. I know this is true! When we recognize this, the guidelines for our spiritual formation become quite simple and compelling:

Love God deeply; do what you can for others; and, please, take good care of yourself.

By keeping these three calls in mind *simultaneously*—even when we are tempted to waiver at times—our inner workshop of virtue will be more apt to stay on the right track, with the right balance and intention. And, as we all know, that is no small thing.

5.

When Invited, Enter the Doorway to Awe

Simplicity is a doorway to the awe that God is constantly inviting us to experience, but we often miss it because our eyes are focused elsewhere. When we are mindful, centered, present, and open—which is what simplicity fosters—we are able to fully receive whatever or whoever is before us without a lot of secular filters or worldly distractions. Rabbi Abraham Joshua Heschel knew this and shared it with his former student, colleague, friend, and fellow rabbi, Samuel Dresner.

Dresner speaks about this in the introduction to the book *I Asked for Wonder*, a collection of some of the writings of Heschel:

> Several years before Abraham Heschel's death in 1972, he suffered a near fatal heart attack from which he never fully recovered. I traveled to his apartment in New York to see him. He had gotten out of bed for the first time to greet me, and was sitting in the living room when I arrived, looking weak and pale. He spoke slowly and with some effort, almost in a whisper. I strained to hear his words.
>
> "Sam," he said, "when I regained consciousness, my first feelings were not of despair or anger. I felt only gratitude to God for my life, for every moment I had lived. I was ready to depart. 'Take me, O Lord,' I thought. 'I have seen so many miracles in my lifetime.'"

Exhausted by the effort, he paused for a moment, then added: "That is what I meant when I wrote [in the preface to his book of

Yiddish poems]: 'I did not ask for success; I asked for wonder. And You gave it to me.'"

Things may happen to us that are the dramatic doorways to wonder and awe. All of us probably have had episodes such as this in which we could almost feel a portal to heaven open and knew that we had just experienced a pronounced display of grace—a miracle of sorts. The following story of a religious sister (a member of the Sisters, Servants of the Immaculate Heart of Mary in Immaculata, Pennsylvania) is an ideal example of this:

> When I was stationed in Cherry Hill, New Jersey, I worked not far from a small, pretty cemetery. Before going to work each day, I took a one-and-a-quarter-mile walk around the cemetery. While I walked, I either prayed the Rosary or just enjoyed the beauty of that sacred ground. On these outings, I never remember pausing at any of the graves.
>
> Then, one day in September, something on a grave across the field caught my eye. Most of the grave sites were decorated with flowers and other signs of grieving and affection, so this one was no different. There was nothing "special" about it at all—even the headstone was quite ordinary.
>
> I passed the site and kept walking, but something drew me back to it. So I finally gave in and walked across to the spot in the middle of the field where the gravestone was. The gravestone was engraved with the person's name, date of birth, and date of death. I noticed right away that the anniversary of her death was just three days away. The stone was the kind that had a place for a picture of the person, so I lifted the cover on it. I saw a beautiful, young woman smiling at me and under the picture the words: "Scholar, Athlete, Loving Daughter." Attached to the stone was also a letter, in plastic, from the woman's grandmother. It was a dear note expressing great love . . . and great loss.
>
> I felt drawn to that stone that day and felt I was there for a reason. So I stayed long enough to offer a prayer for the young woman and her family. Then I left the cemetery to head for work at the parish office.

Later that day, my phone buzzed, and the secretary asked me to speak to a woman who had a question about the use of our church. The pastor was away, and she felt the woman needed some kind of answer now. Would I take the call? Not sure what I could do for her, I decided to find out.

As she explained, the woman belonged to an international bereavement group for parents who had lost children. It was an interdenominational group that met every month, and she belonged to the chapter of Camden, New Jersey. Each year the group holds a prayer service in December at one of the local churches. She wondered if it would be possible to use our church for that year's service. She said that she liked the location, and it was helpful that we also had a basement which could be used for a social gathering.

I asked her more about the group and was truly touched by their commitment to one another. As she was telling me about their purpose, she began to cry. She begged my forgiveness but explained that her daughter's anniversary was coming up and she was feeling the loss greatly right now.

After some more conversation, I asked the woman to give me her full name and phone number so I could get back to her after I spoke with the pastor. I really didn't feel there would be a problem and told her so. She was delighted, and as she gave me her name something squeezed my heart upon hearing it. It was the same last name I found on the headstone in the cemetery that morning. It couldn't possibly be . . .

I interrupted the woman and asked where her daughter was buried. It was in that same cemetery! I asked the girl's name and the date of her death. It was the same! I told the woman that I had been at her daughter's grave that very morning. She gasped and began to cry (as did I!). I explained to her about my daily walk and how the grave site had somehow attracted my attention.

I was actually shaking inside and out! This seemed more than a coincidence to me. What are the chances that I would stop at a grave of someone I didn't even know, especially when I didn't make a habit of doing so, and then actually speak to her mother that very day?

The woman told me that she believed it was a sign from God. She was feeling very low and wondering if her daughter was at peace. She had died suddenly from the effects of a diet pill she had been taking. For this woman, there was no closure, no good-bye, no explanations, no answers. She believed now that her daughter truly was at peace.

I met with the woman a few weeks later and had a long conversation with her. I learned more about this wonderful group of people who support one another in their grief. Later, they asked me to talk to their group at one of their monthly meetings. I felt so inadequate! After hearing some of their stories, I didn't know what I could possibly say to people who had suffered so much and yet had reached out to others in so many ways. I had no idea what it was like to bear so much pain. But they were so very welcoming and made me feel comfortable in their company.

I will never forget that day. Nor will I ever forget those wonderful people and the lessons they taught me. It and they were a gift to me, and I store that memory deep in my heart.

"I store that memory deep in my heart." Those concluding words are so important in the spiritual life. We must not only have the ability to see and experience what is dramatic; we must also *remember*. To return to Rabbi Abraham Joshua Heschel, he noted that all of us have these experiences of God's presence. Yet, most of us put them on a shelf like a trophy to gather dust rather than put them in our hearts as Sister did. When we do that, we are changed and made different. The difference is knowing that God has been with us and then feeling compelled to serve others in ways that demonstrate gratitude for receiving such graceful encounters.

Some of the experiences may not seem significant at the time, but they can still hold great power for us in how we lead our lives. In 2001, I was drinking a cup of coffee early in the morning in an open café in central Bangkok following an intense trip into Cambodia. I noticed a young woman who stopped before a small statue of Buddha to place a glass of cold water and to pray. While I was marveling at her devotion, I saw a young, male Thai worker pause to briefly touch a bright orchid blooming in a little nearby garden. Both gestures affected me deeply and guided me toward greater reverence for life and my own Christian faith. When I find myself rushing through life, I recall these brief encounters and slow myself down from rushing to my grave.

The main character in Paulo Coehlo's famous novel, *The Alchemist*, is cautioned about running through his life and thus risking missing the guideposts left him by God. We can slow down and enter the doorway to awe. In the morning, we can take a few moments in silence and solitude, wrapped in gratitude before God. Then we can pause occasionally throughout the day to recall who we are and what our call is. When we do this, we lessen the chances that we will miss God's guideposts. Instead, we will see God's hand in the dramatic and in the everyday—in the quiet falling of snow on snow, in the laughter of a small child, and in the smiling face of someone we love. God will be around and within us; and because of a discerning spirit, we will recognize that the divine is always within reach. We need "just" to open our eyes, reach out, and see differently. But to do this, of course, we must have developed a finely tuned reflective spirit, which is certainly one of the key activities in a workshop of virtue.

6.

Cultivate a Reflective Spirit

Sometimes spiritual discernment, the ability to distinguish what is truly good, is fairly easy. The situation presents itself, and you know immediately what to do. Several years ago, one of my granddaughters called and said, "Pop-Pop, I'm in the fourth grade now. Starting in the fifth grade they no longer have special person's day. This is my last chance to have you come out to Wisconsin from Maryland to be at my side at the school for this event. *Will you come?*" And—even though I was due at a conference in Phoenix, Arizona, soon after my granddaughter's event—I, of course, made a Wisconsin detour on the way.

Yet, many times we are presented with situations that aren't as clear. There is no one right answer to the life puzzle that in Japanese is referred to as a *koan*. For instance, we might have two nephews, one having a problem with addiction, another (his brother) almost ignored by his parents because he is doing so well. As an aunt or uncle, which one should we spend the most time with? Questions such as this confront us all the time—many with no obvious single answer.

Discernment is usually not clear-cut. It is dependent on God's grace and is not merely the simple result of careful calculation. However, there are some basic questions that are worth considering when we look to the future. It is important to be aware of these key questions as we face choices in life. Our responses may well determine not only what we do in little things but how we will live our entire life. This is especially so during those key wisdom years after forty that are so precious to us and those with whom we journey in our family and circle of friends, as well as others we encounter at work or in ministry.

Being spiritually reflective is an ongoing process. It happens during the day as we are faced with both large and seemingly small choices. During those moments, we must remember the lessons we have been taught from scripture and our faith tradition. In addition, as we make moral and ethical choices, the counsel of good friends is invaluable.

Discerning the future is not simply a process of weighing pros and cons and seeing how a choice might affect us financially, psychologically, or professionally. It is also about recognizing that while the voices of culture, self-interest, politics, and our professions may be good, they must also be put into perspective so they don't drown out the voice of God.

The voice of God is not often a booming one, but it can still be heard if we take steps to be attuned to it. When we have a sense of expectancy and openness, we may hear God's voice during quiet prayer, in the midst of an encounter, or through the voice of a mentor. Such occurrences awaken us to look for clarity in ways that we could not have previously imagined.

Once when I was taking a walk along the Shenandoah River with my mentor, I was interested in what he thought about a decision that I was facing, and I asked him for his opinion. In response, he surprised me by asking, "Well, what does your wife think?" My first unspoken reaction was, "What does that have to do with it? This is a discernment about what *I* might or might not do." However, since he was my mentor, I simply told him what she had said when we discussed the alternatives before me. He replied, "That sounds about right. Follow her intuition on this." And so, knowing and truly entertaining the wisdom of two people I trusted, I did.

Funny how we hear but don't really listen to what God is telling us through so many sources. Maybe if we didn't prejudge, we would be better discerners. Consider the following questions:

- When do we turn a blind eye to what our children are trying to show us?
- How often is something that is said in passing missed—something that could perhaps have pointed us in the right direction?
- When are we so full of our own ego, opinions, and ways of doing things that there is no space to unlearn something that no longer works?

Being a discerning person is not so much knowing a lot of techniques but having an open mind—what some spiritual guides call "beginner's mind." When we have such humility, there is much we can learn about where God is calling us to go next, what to do, who to be. Without such an outlook, we may lead a good life, but we will miss the greater possibilities that life offers. Those missed possibilities are a real loss, not only for us, but those who turn to us for guidance and support.

7.

Avoid "Spiritual Alzheimer's"

Another virtue as rare as humility—and often absent in its pure form or misunderstood in some way—is gratitude. The need for gratitude is evident in the powerful New Testament parable of the ten lepers. Ten are cured; only one returns to give thanks.

In terms of gratitude, nothing has changed today. Hundreds of thousands of letters to Santa Claus are written every year. Every post office is inundated with them. But how many thank-you notes for gifts received are sent to Santa *after* Christmas? Most post offices would reply that there are none.

In his classic work, *Gratefulness, the Heart of Prayer*, Brother David Steindl-Rast writes the following about this essential virtue:

> Even the predictable turns into surprise the moment we stop taking it for granted. . . . Surprise is no more than a beginning of that fullness we call gratefulness. But a beginning it is. Do we find it difficult to imagine that gratefulness could ever become our basic attitude toward life? In moments of surprise we catch at least a glimpse of the joy to which gratefulness opens the door. More than that—in moments of surprise we already have a foot in the door.

Some people fear being grateful because they then will feel indebted to those who have given them so much. Others are not grateful because they take for granted what they have and want more. One of the greatest enemies of the spiritual life—and, in turn, of living with a sense of contentment, peace, and joy—is *entitlement*. With this, we are always looking for more or feeling deprived of what we think is our just desserts. This is sad because all of life is a gift. Without gratitude, our souls run the risk of becoming hardened. We overlook the blessings we already have yet deem of little worth.

There is so much to celebrate in our lives, both in the past and in the present, that the problem should be deciding where to begin in giving thanks. Our society pretends to hold the copyright on selling happiness and constantly tells us what others have and we lack. The goal is to foster a culture of consumers who are always grasping for more. Jealousy and envy are the commodities on which a secular society thrives. In a spiritual community, though, the goal is to uncover what is already there that we are missing.

Gratefulness also slows us down and helps us live more reflective, prayerful lives. This is especially important today when we are so busy—even with doing good things—that we miss the very gifts of God that would help us to continue to do what is helpful for others. Once again, Brother David offers insight in his reflection on how Jesus invites us to "behold the lilies of the field":

> The do-gooder is too busy. He has no time to bother with flowers. With six tongues the glory of God shouts at us from every lily in bloom, "Stop and look!" Or, as the Psalm puts it, "Be still and know" (Ps 46:10). But the busybody does not understand the language of their silent eloquence. He rushes on: "Sorry, I don't speak Lily." His ears are buzzing with the din of his own projects, ideas, and good intentions.

So what should be our response if we wish to open ourselves to a spirit of deeper gratefulness? *Surprise.* Brother David recognizes that most of us leave the house each day with a preformed sense of what we should be grateful for. He suggests we throw away this list and be open to whatever comes our way. But to do this, we must first be willing to *let go.*

8.

Honor the Spirituality of Letting Go

Being open to new perspectives is especially important as we move through different stages and are called to turn natural or unforeseen corners in life. Letting go facilitates this process. Still, it is not easy, because of habits, fears, and past hurtful experiences. Lily Tomlin is once purported to have exclaimed, "Forgiveness means giving up all hope of a better past."

Letting go means catching ourselves in the act of holding on to a feeling or reaction that is not from a good place within ourselves. A psychotherapist who is also a member of a religious order once shared with me, "When I find myself being tempted to be small-minded or mean-spirited, I remind myself of the invitation to be magnanimous, where I find my better self." This better self is one that is more open, one that doesn't deny difficulties but also doesn't see things in polarities of right and wrong or good and bad. The better self is able to be receptive to a richer and more nuanced experience of life.

Letting go is often resisted because we feel we are going to lose something rather than gain something greater. When we do let go, we gain the inner freedom to experience so much more. In holding on, we miss all that we can experience because we have overly centered on one thing or person. In his book with the intriguing title *The Crooked Cucumber*, David Chadwick tells the story of a monk staring intently at a beautiful piece of pottery and being told by his abbot, "Stop committing adultery." Since the monastery had no women in it, of course he was not speaking about the monk's being sexually promiscuous. What he was addressing is the fact that the monk was not simply enjoying looking and admiring a beautiful creation but instead was becoming attached to it with a desire to possess it. Anthony de Mello put it this way:

> If you look carefully you will see that there is one thing and only one thing that causes unhappiness. The name of that is attachment. What is attachment? An emotional state of clinging caused by the belief that without some particular thing or some person you cannot be happy.

Once again, this does not mean that we cannot enjoy people, things, and occurrences in life. Far from that, we can see that those whom we admire for their selfless work are the very ones who completely embrace what they have been given. They are not captured by their appreciation of their gifts in a way that makes them feel as if they can no longer serve or that they must have something in particular in life as a price for their own happiness.

This is the case with letting go of our opinions and habits as well—we can benefit by valuing them without being too attached. If we are to accomplish such a "letting go" in this arena, we need a sense of prayerfulness and spiritual awareness that allows us to zoom out and see a bigger picture. Things are not as straightforward as they seem. Once in the Foreign Correspondents Club in Phnom Penh in Cambodia, I sat at a table looking out over the Mekong River and felt a sense of peace and timelessness. But soon, as the noonday heat began to steam up, the restaurant proprietor opened the slatted windows on the other side of the room to let a breeze come through. On this side, I could see the old walls of the buildings deeper in the city; they were marked by bullet holes still there from the days of the Khmer Rouge. Which scene was true? Both of them were.

If we are to let go and greet new attitudes, possibilities, and broader ways of viewing events, experiences, others, and—yes—even ourselves, we must be willing to move into the uncertain, gray areas of life. It is in this spiritual and psychological space that we can experience so much more if we let go.

Philip Simmons, who contracted ALS, also known as Lou Gehrig's disease, spoke about this in terms of more ultimate "letting go" experiences in his book, *Learning to Fall*:

> I can't hike the high mountain ridges anymore, I tell myself, but I can take my wheelchair out on a mountain road and smell the balsam fir. It's all a matter of perspective, we like to say. (What does the snail say when riding on the turtle's back? "Whee!") But I've learned the hard way that too often the comfort provided by such thoughts resembles the brief high I get from eating chocolate; soon after, I plunge into irritability and depression. The approach I've found more helpful is also more difficult. It is born out of a paradox: that we deal most fruitfully with loss by accepting the fact that we will one day lose everything. When we learn to fall, we learn that only by letting go our grip on all that we ordinarily find most precious—our achievements, our plans, our loved ones, our very selves—can we find, ultimately, the most profound freedom. In the act of letting go of our lives, we return more fully to them.

This is one of the core spiritual tenets given to us by Christ: "Whoever tries to hold onto his life, loses it. Whoever loses his life for my sake, saves it." What this means to us and how we live out of a life of freedom—in which we are not grasping but enjoying, not collecting but sharing—will determine much about the level of maturity one's personal inner formation has reached.

9.

Mine the Wisdom of Spiritual Sadness

Author H. G. Wells once said that he wouldn't describe himself as an unhappy man. Nevertheless, he reported that he never felt completely safe from periodic attacks of acute misery. Many of us might not put it quite so dramatically; yet, without warning, feelings of sadness can seem to come when we least expect them.

I am not speaking here about clinical depression or a significant "dark night of the soul"—both of which are rare, rather pronounced feelings. When I speak of *spiritual* sadness, I am referring to those melancholic periods that seem to find us amid our normal routine. They may stop us in our tracks for a few short moments, an hour—or, on occasion, for a full day or longer—without any discernible or apparent cause. They may be prompted by a thought, memory, short interaction, or e-mail. Yet, if we honor them properly, they can teach us a great deal. We only need to look in the proper way. Such is certainly the case with respect to what we perceive to be negative feedback from others.

As an overly sensitive person much too concerned about my image or reputation, criticism never falls lightly when it is dropped on me. Being before the public because of my writings, presentations, courses, and numerous interactions doesn't make it any easier; it only increases the chances of disappointing people. However, since I am passionate about being involved—what I call "looking over the wall of life"—I need to constantly open space within my personality style and vulnerabilities in order to learn, grow, and hopefully become more compassionate toward others, including those who gave me feedback that is difficult for me to face or at times even fathom.

This is the case when the negative reaction floods my emotions, especially when I am tired or on the road and particularly caught off-guard. I might have such immediate reactions as, "How could someone react so disapprovingly to a presentation I had spent so much time preparing?" "How could he or she so greatly misjudge my motives and be so vindictive in his or her comments?" Or, "Why would someone who I valued leave such a hurtful message on my phone or e-mail?" The list goes on and on for me, and I know for others, too. Still, such sadness, feelings of being misunderstood, or guilt about something inadvertently said or done need not be the final spiritual word. The sadness and upset initially caused can actually lead to wisdom if we gently hold our personal faults in one hand and the possibility for new learning in the other.

Sadness becomes spiritual when we realize that it is not the final word. It is actually an opening to new freedom from what would quietly dictate the wrong messages to our heart. If this is to happen though, we must be willing to fully experience the feeling, thoughts, and beliefs that lie below the surface. These are what are nailing us to the cross of our own egos and destructive or dysfunctional thinking. Within the sadness itself, there is a desire for freedom from what is causing it in your own heart. For this desire to grow, we must provide it with space and whatever moments of mindfulness we may find in the course of the day.

In his book *Ten Poems to Change Your Life*, poetry devotee Roger Housden writes:

> You may not have a name for your heart's desire; you may not even recognize it as a spiritual yearning. It may be some persistent discomfort with your life that you have not known how to respond to, or some inexplicable melancholy that comes upon you some evenings and leaves the next morning. Changing jobs or marriage partners doesn't make it go away. Yet that uncomfortable itch is the

raft that will carry you across the ocean. Instead of acting it out—plunging into extreme sports, wild affairs, obsessive money-making—you can allow yourself to experience it.

You can feel it, the tangible ache in the chest; you can let it carry you deeper than your thoughts about yourself, deeper than your ideas about spirituality and the meaning of life, down into the spacious simplicity, the silence that is the root of your being. Being present to yourself is the beginning of a journey without end. That kind of journey is itself the destination. All you are asked to do is to start down that road.

When we take the time to examine our sadness further—beyond projecting blame on others, beyond castigating ourselves, beyond discouragement because there is no immediate fix for it—then we are opening ourselves up to a journey that is filled with much wisdom and possibility. The question is: Will we?

10.

Adjust Your Inner Lens

Perception is a blend of fact and fiction. Personal formation, if it is to be effective, seeks to minimize what is not true—even though we may wish it were. Through gentle clarity we can uncover what is accurate about a situation, person, event, or ourselves. The most complete picture can emerge.

When we are in touch with the truth about ourselves and the world, we can find healing. But we must proceed in an evenhanded way. In one hand there must be clarity and in the other, kindness. If there is too much clarity, we can be hurtful to ourselves. Psychologists call this a "narcissistic injury." If there is too much kindness, there is no growth. The balance needs to be there.

What helps in this regard is to have a circle of friends whose values are Christian—not simply in words, for anyone can say what they claim to believe. Their Christianity must be evident in the way they live their lives. In the past, I have recommended at least four types of friends or "voices" that need to be present for the feedback, support, challenge, and inspiration we need:

- *The Prophet* asks us what voices are guiding us in life. So often we move through life thinking we are aware and in control of what we are feeling, thinking, and doing, but unrecognized influences from the past are there as invisible puppeteers pulling our strings.

- *The Cheerleader* is a supportive and sympathetic individual. This type of person is there to listen to our woes and encourage us on.
- *The Harasser or Teaser* helps us keep perspective through the use of humor and friendly teasing so that, in the process of taking what is important in life seriously, we don't take ourselves too seriously instead.
- *The Inspirational or Spiritual Friend* calls us to be all that we can be without embarrassing us because we are where we are now.

There also must be a vulnerability and nondefensiveness in how we embrace our feelings. This is part of adjusting our inner lens. Once again in the words of psychologist and spiritual guide Jack Kornfield:

> The emotional wisdom of the heart is simple. When we accept our human feelings, a remarkable transformation occurs. Tenderness and wisdom arise naturally and spontaneously. Where we once sought strength over others, now our strength becomes our own; where we once sought to defend ourselves we laugh.

When we have such an approach, our mind is like a clean mirror, reflecting what is, not what we would like or what others have determined. The mirror for us should be our emotions, and the clarity of the mirror is impacted significantly by our unexamined thoughts and beliefs. This is why, each evening, a spiritual debriefing is a good idea.

To do it is very simple and powerful. It involves some very basic steps. The following is an example of one approach:

1. Find a quiet space by yourself. It could be during a walk after work or dinner, during a ride home, or in a separate space in your house.
2. Walk yourself through the day from the time you got up. As you review this "movie of your day," write down the peaks and valleys as well as anything surprising that happened.

3. Once you have done this, go over them and note in a word or two—either mentally or on paper—your feelings and thoughts about what happened. Be nonjudgmental; don't pick on yourself or others, and catch yourself if you are getting discouraged. The goal is not to solve anything but to observe without any interference from your ego, your needs, or anything else. Keep the fluency going by simply being intrigued by what you are observing.

4. Review the cognitions (ways of thinking, perceiving, and understanding) that arise, and examine them for their validity or any distortions you may have introduced. Such distortions may be through exaggeration and personalization of some perceived failure—for instance, "because I made a mistake, I am a mistake." Gently respond to unhelpful, inaccurate, distorted thinking without picking on yourself for thinking that way. Also, catch yourself when you are projecting the blame on others. It may feel good to blame others for your problems, but when you give away the blame, you also give away the power to change. Most of the power to change, clinical and spiritual evidence has shown, is within *you*.

5. Finally, in light of your spiritual values, faith, and theology, ask what you have learned from this and how you would like to change personally and in your compassionate and ministerial actions with others. If there is no change within you or in your actions, such activities are really pointless.

6. After this, a prayer of thanksgiving to God for the learning through the day's events is an ideal way to close. It is a way to acknowledge that all of life is our spiritual director—even the difficult people we meet and events that befall us—when we are open to walking through them with God.

When we do this, we will learn from the emotional residue of the day. Rather than being simply an exercise in finding comfort, pleasure, and praise, or in avoiding pain, conflict, and disagreeable events, life will be more—much more. It will be a spiritual journey into becoming more and more wise and compassionate, and it will bear fruits of peace, balance, clarity, and true joy.

II.

Discover Both Your Gifts and Growing Edges

A spiritual mentor once said to his disciples, "You are all perfect as you are . . . and you could all use a little improvement." Like my granddaughters, whom I mentioned earlier, we can all name things we are particularly good at, our "signature strengths." We only need to actualize them. This can be done by accepting ourselves just as we are, while also calling ourselves to become who we can be.

Even the most talented person has challenges to bear. Conversely, even the most challenged individual has many—often untapped— gifts to recognize, develop, and share. Swiss psychiatrist Carl Jung knew this was the case and felt that everyone is challenged according to his or her abilities, or in his own words, "The brighter the light, the deeper the darkness."

Psychology has often focused almost solely on the negative aspects of personality. More frequently than not, this has also been an error prevalent in spiritual-formation programs. The focus now in both psychology and spirituality is shifting so that attention is given to a person's gifts, talents, and virtues—all of which are important for living a balanced, full, and compassionate life. God is calling us to build on what is good and not merely focus on our sins. It is not that we shouldn't view our sins; the problem is when we look at them too exclusively and ignore the gifts God has given us to enjoy and share with others.

In his book *Authentic Happiness*, Martin Seligman, who initiated the positive psychology movement, states:

> The field of positive psychology at the subjective level is about positive subjective experience: well-being and satisfaction (past); flow, joy, the sensual pleasures, and happiness (present); and constructive cognitions about the future—optimism, hope, and faith. At the individual level it is about positive personality traits—the capacity for love and vocation, forgiveness, originality, future-mindedness, high talent, and wisdom. . . Psychology is not just the study of disease, weakness, and damage; it also is the study of strength and virtue. Treatment is not just fixing what is wrong; it also is building what is right. . . the major strides in prevention have largely come from a perspective focused on systematically building competency, not correcting weakness.

The same can be said of spirituality. Rather than focusing simply on one's sins or what is going wrong, there must be an emphasis as well on what is going right. Once we see clearly the gifts God has given us, then we can identify those situations where these very gifts are exaggerated or minimized. If you are an inspirational person, maybe when you feel threatened you become more egotistical and thus dominate conversations. Or possibly you are a great listener and tend to be quiet. When feeling threatened, you may not say anything at all and thus deprive those around you of your thoughts and feelings—the very information that is counted on to build up others.

In personal formation, the goal must be to look at both gifts and growing edges. To do this, it is essential to be nonjudgmental of ourselves during the process of self-examination. One way to accomplish this is to begin with a recognition of a full list of our gifts. This is not being narcissistic, because they are gifts from God and as such need to be recognized, owned, and developed. Then we can both enjoy them and share them freely with others, expecting nothing in return. By doing this first and then looking at our sins or mistakes and the situations that serve to increase them, we engage in a proper exercise in self-understanding and self-transformation, not self-condemnation. In the end, self-condemnation does nothing.

12.

Expand Your Rituals of Reverence

There is another important question that we need to ask ourselves during this inner workshop: What rituals do we need in order to transform our awareness of our lives from being a bundle of trivial, practical chores into an actual pilgrimage—even during the performance of mundane tasks?

While on a trip to Boston, my wife and I went to Mass at St. Paul's Church near Harvard Square. The choir provided amazingly uplifting music, and the atmosphere was one of powerful joy and reverent adoration. After Mass, we went to breakfast before moving on to the purpose of our trip. During breakfast, I told my wife that I was deeply moved by the liturgy and felt I could no longer continue to go to Mass as I had in the past. I needed good liturgy that included carefully prepared homilies that were scripture based and mature in their delivery. I needed a community that I could be a part of and music I could join in and feel that I had one foot in the particulars of this world and one in the infinite setting of the next. In other words, I needed a ritual of renewal each week that was eucharistic, sensitive to the Word of God, and conducive to being touched by the lives of those around me. When we returned home, we began to travel about forty minutes each way to a Carmelite monastery in Baltimore for Sunday liturgy.

However, this was not the end. It was the beginning for me because it sensitized me to how other rituals during the day, week, and life in general might reinforce a sense of reverence for what is truly important and life-giving. When such things came my way, I wanted to truly experience them rather than be oblivious to them.

One such experience that captured my attention happened in a small café in Wellington, New Zealand. I was there to spend some time with the priests and religious educators of the diocese and also to address the New Zealand Psychological Association. Following one of the presentations, the hosts took me out for dinner. During the meal, the Maori guitar player who was entertaining and instructing us on the culture of his people asked us to join in a traditional Maori song. As we did this, I heard a fine baritone voice of another man, also American, who was at another table. His voice carried to our table and harmonized with us. I could feel, not only the depth of the Maori people in it, but a sense of community that only song and music can convey. The question it raised in my mind concerned whether I was aware enough of how music can be a ritual of reverence. It awakened me to music's potential to go around or break through the cognitive envelope of thought that I often live in and to enable me truly to experience the presence of God *now*.

Like liturgy and music, there are other rituals of reverence that we can employ. These might include a quiet period in the morning, a reflection at different times during the day, or a meal with friends. The important thing is that we look at our schedule and life to see what rituals we can develop that bring us closer to God, each other, life, and ourselves. In retiring from or changing jobs, saying good-bye through rituals can offer closure and an opportunity to understand, let go, and open up to what is before us. In modern society, rituals have fallen by the wayside, but the need for them hasn't.

You can see that reflected in what happens when a movie star or someone attractive in the public eye dies. Such funerals are watched by people who have never even met the deceased. Flowers are left in places where the person has lived or died. A true desire to be part of the person's life and to ritualize their death in one's own life is felt by so many. Why? Because those very rituals of connection, those sacraments of life, are often absent today. And so reviewing our rituals and strengthening them needs to be part of life and certainly part of a personal spiritual formation program.

13.

Welcome the Softening Place of Humor

In Penelope Rowlands's edited work *Paris Was Ours*, the contributors describe the experiences both wondrous and challenging, uplifting and demeaning, that they encountered as writers from other countries living in France. One of them, Natasha Fraser-Cavassoni, said that learning to adjust to acerbic, possibly stinging humor was one of the travails she had to endure. In one instance, she asked a middle-aged man for directions, and the response was, "Mademoiselle, do I look like a map?"

People who have a good sense of humor tend to be nondefensive and open to feedback. I remember once sharing with a priest, who eventually became a bishop, that the vocations office that I was involved with at the time was going to send him a seminarian for pastoral supervision. He said to me, "Is there a special reason you are sending him to me?" In response, I teased, "Well, he is very stubborn, but you are even more stubborn, so I thought it would work out well." He smiled broadly and exclaimed, "Well, how did you ever know that about me? I thought I kept it a secret!" And we both laughed.

Michael Mott, in his book *The Seven Mountains of Thomas Merton*, pointed out how this well-known contemplative and writer was able to laugh at himself more and more as he matured. We see this capacity in people we admire. Hopefully, we too can laugh at ourselves. When we cannot, we suffer, but so do those around us.

When we can't laugh at ourselves and our foibles, it is usually part of a greater wall of defensiveness. One top American political leader, known for his sarcasm and belittling comments about others who disagreed with him, was on a national morning show as part of a publicity campaign for his recently published book. When asked what mistakes he had made while in office, he brushed the question aside, saying that if he answered, some people would only pounce on it as a way of fostering their own agendas. When people at the top of government can't admit to errors, it is sad. As we seek to find God and ourselves more deeply, the inability to laugh at ourselves is not only sad—it may turn out to be sinful. Given our goal, I am not sure which is worse.

14.

Establish a "Little Rule" of Your Own

Jack Kornfield writes about a spiritual teacher who was asked about the beautiful faith and warmth he radiated. His students said, "This is what we want from you. How do we learn that?" In response, according to Kornfield, the spiritual guide "described how he practiced year after year, living simply, hearing the same teachings over and over again, sitting [in quiet prayer] no matter what," and following a spiritual rule.

The spiritual life is not to be taken lightly. By this I don't mean that we should be unduly serious. What I mean is that we should have a way to ensure that we don't slip into drifting through life and, in the process, miss its essence. Like the spiritual teacher that Kornfield mentions, we too need a "little rule" of life.

In the fourth and fifth centuries, the *Abbas* (fathers) and *Ammas* (mothers) of the desert developed a rule of prayer for themselves. The rule included liturgy, formal prayers, reading and reflecting on scripture, meditation, contemplation, appointed times for reflection, conversation with God, and faith sharing. Today our "little rules" might include activities similar to those of the desert rule, but also contemporary practices such as journaling, listening to sacred music (or other music conducive to prayer), drawing, and being mindful to God's presence while walking, eating, or during any activity.

The goal of having a rule is to exchange *chronos*, a secular way of viewing time, for *chairos*, a way of seeing time through the eyes of God. The goal is not to be more religious. Rather, it is to prevent our faith from becoming domesticated or captured by secular values and promises. In essence, the purpose of a "little rule" of prayer is to help us live our lives prayerfully and to be more fully aware of all of life. Then we can share these rules openly with others in the same spirit that we received them freely from God.

The development of a "little rule" of prayer usually begins slowly. A person will include Sunday liturgy as a way to meet God in the Eucharist, to hear the Word of God in the gospel and the other scripture readings, and to encounter Christ in others. Following this, one may find that having quiet periods for reflection and meditation are strong, silent, simple ways to let the scaffolding of the world fall aside. Some get up a bit early, take a walk during lunchtime, don't turn on the radio during the ride home, or take some time out in the evening after all have gone to sleep.

The Rosary, reading scripture for ten minutes or so, attending a novena to the Blessed Mother, participating in a Bible study, visiting a friend who enjoys speaking about the spiritual life, and so on can all be part of a "little rule." The list can be endless, but it needs to be one that is realistic given your schedule and preferences. Once that list is developed and followed, then further insight as to how it may be deepened or expanded may occur. Also, the search for a spiritual director to meet with about every six weeks might also come about as a way to ensure the path taken is the best one possible given the realities of your situation, personality, and spiritual maturity.

The simple initial goal is to form the rule and follow it. Once that occurs, then further steps for deepening, expanding, or changing it will become clear. The important first step, though, is that the goal to develop and use a rule of prayer must not just stay in the planning stage but should be acted upon now.

15.

Understand the Important Role of Death . . . While You're Still Alive!

The possibility of death is with us from birth. Then one day it either drops on us violently or, as is more often the case, lightly taps us on the shoulder and tells us it will soon be *our* time to leave. Knowing this deeply—not just theoretically—helps us become less petty and more gratefully compassionate to others. Yet, if you were to bring up this helpful reality at a social gathering, the response would normally be a shiver, a laugh—or worse, a derisive comment rather than a word of thanks. This reaction may well be a culturally conditioned Western one.

Michel de Montaigne, in his *Selected Essays*, tells of a tribe in Africa that puts a skull on the table during celebrations. This is done so people may recognize that their time on this earth is limited and so value even more the joy of being with others and the meal before them. Richard Bode puts it this way in his book *First You Have to Row a Little Boat*: "The day will come when I will die. So, the only matter of consequence before me is what I will do with my allotted time. I can remain on shore, paralyzed with fear, or I can raise my sails and dip and soar in the breeze."

Keeping death before us in morning and evening prayer and allowing death to accompany us during the day helps us to maintain

48

a proper perspective. When we realize that we are dying and so is everyone else, we tend to be less demeaning, demanding, or hard to please. We will also let our kindness take root and even deal well with difficult people. We will realize that those who use unpalatable defenses have to live with themselves and that this is the best they can do at the moment. Keeping death before us changes everything.

16.

Be More Attuned to the Power of Your Attitude and Self-Talk

Psychology teaches us that through our personality, cognitions (i.e., ways of thinking, perceiving, and understanding), and our self-talk we will find either suffering or joy. Spirituality echoes this understanding but brings it to a greater sense of meaning. If the voice we hear in self-talk is inspired by a deep sense of God's love for us and our love for all those we meet, then we will have a sense of invitation rather than judgment. Our self-talk will foster hope, have us meet the right challenges, and help us be compassionate toward all—including ourselves in tough moments.

Martha Gellhorn, who was married to the author Ernest Hemingway, is quoted by Caroline Moorehead in her book *Gellhorn* as saying, "I am entranced by the furious miseries people make for themselves in their own heads." Once again, Jack Kornfield adds to this something very relevant to personal inner formation when he notes:

> As we undertake to quiet our minds through meditation or prayer, we see how much of our lives are governed by . . . unconscious stories. . . . We begin to see the themes of our inner dialogue, which can be ambition or unworthiness, insecurity or hope, self-hatred or self-improvement. The stories reflect our conditioning, personal

and cultural. . . . Central to the stories we tell are the fixed beliefs we have about ourselves. . . . . Because those thoughts and assumptions are so powerful, we live out their energies over and over. . . . An honorable [spiritual] practice unmasks these stories and releases their limiting beliefs. . . . We begin . . . to learn that they are not the most fundamental reality.

As I noted a number of years ago in my own book *Seeds of Sensitivity*, having accurate self-talk as we walk through the day is not just about us. Once we have a more correct sense of self—because we have examined our self-talk to ensure we are neither projecting the blame on others, picking on ourselves, nor being unrealistic to the point of discouragement—then we can be more free and more integrated. We can be as sensitive to all people as we are to ourselves. This will save energy and help us to develop as persons. We will stop wasting energy trying to deal with the incorrect, often exaggerated things we tell ourselves during the day.

With a real sense of self that comes from accurately seeing situations and discussing them nonjudgmentally within ourselves, we can approach situations with a greater sense of certainty and humility. Consequently, rather than seeking approval or reinforcement, we act out of a truer identity of ourselves and greater self-knowledge about both our gifts and growing edges.

When we can feel ourselves becoming anxious, depressed, or under stress, we can ask ourselves questions that will bring us back in touch with our central identity before God. Such questions will help us see that our fears or "dis-ease" are arising out of trying to play a role, fearing rejection, or being revealed in some ways as a charlatan or bad person. They will allow us to face the familiar as well as the unfamiliar, the attractive as well as the unattractive, and the challenging as well as the comforting with a sense of equanimity. When that occurs, we will find that we don't inordinately overestimate or underestimate ourselves. We will seek to learn in all situations and feel the freedom that comes when we don't need so much energy for defense or offense. We will become less concerned about our image before others or even some ideal image we have for ourselves. Instead, we'll become more focused on simply being a friend of God. As Jesus tells us, "I have called you friends" (Jn 15:15).

17.

Practice Faithfulness . . . and Let God Take Care of the Residue

Sometimes we get upset when we look at all the suffering in the world. But at other times, what upsets us is the annoying people around us. We wish that someone in our family, circle of friends, work, parish, or religious community would change and become better. We have tried to be helpful, but the situation doesn't change. One of the results is that their problem becomes our problem.

When we are feeling troubled, worried, and tired, asking ourselves some simple questions can be very helpful. Among some examples are the following:

- When we are seeking to be compassionate to others, are we including *ourselves*? Self-compassion is a sign of self-respect. That is not only what we are called to do by God, but it is a wonderful attitude to model for those around us who are troubled.
- Are we more concerned about being personally faithful to doing what we can for others than about success or appreciation? The only person who can change someone is that person.
- Do we follow these steps (especially the fifth one): (1) recognize the challenges in life, (2) decide on what we feel is the source of them, (3) plan what to do, (4) do what we can, and in the end (5) *let God take care of the residue*? If we could take that fifth step at

the end of each day, imagine how much deeper our sleep would be—and how much more peaceful our lives would be.

When we focus on faithfulness—doing what we can when we can—rather than on success, the amount of frustration we will feel will be much less. This will then have many benefits. We will feel less frustrated when things don't go as we wish they would. There will be less chance that the person we are trying to help will feel that we are forcing them to do something. It will lessen the danger that we will think ill of persons we are trying to help because they are not improving as quickly as *we* would like them to. And finally, and of no little consequence, we will avoid the "savior complex" by recognizing what is in our hands and what is in God's hands.

This last point is so important because as religious people we often proclaim we have faith in God. Yet, when there is a difficult situation, we put it all on human shoulders—be it ours or others. It is not that we should not do what we can in challenging situations where we can have a positive role. The question we must confront as a part of our personal inner-formation efforts is: Do we have enough faith to let God take care of the residue?

18.

Savor Some Silence Each Day

One of the most gratifying trips I have ever taken was to South Africa to speak on resilience. And one of the most enjoyable parts of this journey was during the break between my presentations in Johannesburg and Cape Town to take a brief photographic safari in the Sabi Sands on the edge of Kruger National Park. In the morning, my wife and I joined others in an open Range Rover for a three-hour trip into thousands of acres of protected-wildlife area.

It was winter at the time, quite cool, and we were wrapped up in blankets with a hot water bottle to warm our hands. As we drove quite quickly across the open veld at the start of the journey, I could see the heads of giraffe above some of the trees. I was amazed at the quiet that seemed to envelope me, and I smiled silently at the small herd of agile springbok jumping in the distance. Although our goal was to see lions, elephants, Cape buffalo, rhinos, and hippos (and we did), this one early-morning moment was worth a trip halfway around the world. There is something about the feel of silence and being enveloped in a quiet wind that takes one's breath away.

Author and literary critic Doris Grumbach wrote in her book *Fifty Days of Solitude* about her experience of time alone in a way that helps me understand its value better:

> There was a reward for [silence and solitude]. The absence of other voices compelled me to listen more intently to the inner one. I

became aware that the interior voice, so often before stifled or stilted by what I thought others wanted to hear, or what I considered to be socially acceptable, grew gratifyingly louder, more insistent. . . . My intention was to discover what was in there . . . [a] treasure of fresh insight?

Yet, Grumbach is also realistic about the doubt and hesitation that many experience when alone or quiet for an extended period of time. She added later on in the book:

How right Rousseau was about the modern person. Our points of reference are always our neighbors, the people in the village or our city, our acquaintances at school, at games, at work, our close and distant friends, all of whom tell us, with their hundreds of tongues, who we are. . . . Rarely if ever did we think to look within for knowledge of ourselves. Were we afraid? Perhaps, we thought we would find nothing there."

Still, even forced solitude can bear fruit if we eventually open ourselves to it and the silence we experience in such situations. A person sent to prison in England surprised people when upon his release he indicated that he never minded the twenty years taken away from him. He felt that he probably would have wasted those years had he not been imprisoned. He then went on to share that he had not expected to miss anything about prison upon his release, but he did miss the good deal of reading and meditation he did while in jail. Those experiences brought him peace, a peace not readily found in the noisy, busy world where he now found himself.

When we embark on an inner workshop to foster our spiritual formation, silence and solitude are part of the rule of prayer we set out for ourselves. We seek to find some time during the day—even if it is only for a few moments—to sit quietly, gently clear our mind, look at an icon or something inspirational, and possibly use a centering word such as "Jesus," "gentleness," or another word that has deep meaning for us.

In doing this, we try to establish set times so the day does not sweep away these essential periods that center us and bring us home to God and ourselves. However, we also need to look for the crumbs of "alonetime" (time in solitude or within ourselves when we are in a group) outside of these periods. It may be on a short walk at noon, when we are sipping a cup of coffee or tea alone in our office or kitchen, or during a drive home. The possibilities are endless, as are the places we can seek out: corners of libraries, churches, small city parks, a nearby forest preserve, or a jogging path. If we have a value system that savors some silence in our lives, the crumbs of alonetime can be quite nourishing. But we have to find them.

19.

Emulate the Right Persons to Follow the Path of Grace

When we were in elementary school, our parents probably gave us a lecture at some point on the importance of good friends. They could lift us up or lead us astray. When we become adults and feel we are in control, there is a tendency to set aside our parents' admonition. However, the situation has not changed. The type of friends we have can truly have an impact for good or bad, no matter how old we are.

In his book *Merton and Friends*, James Harford quoted Merton as saying that he was taught to "imitate not Rockefeller but Thoreau. . . . I ended up being turned on like a pinball machine by Blake, Thomas Aquinas, Augustine, Eckhart, Commeraswamy, Traherne, Hopkins, Maritain, and the sacraments of the Catholic Church." In line with this, Harford noted that Merton's best friend also echoed this sentiment in saying, "We felt we could do something that was going in the opposite direction from the whole commercial world. We'd already had brushes with that world, and we didn't like it."

Of the people in our circle of friends, there is usually one whom we consider to be a mentor. This person may have an especially important impact on how we live our lives. And so the type of person that is and how we choose to avail ourselves of the wisdom being offered in this relationship is important.

In the chapter "On Being a Desert Apprentice" in my book *Crossing the Desert,* one of the objectives I had was to list some of the attributes of a potential mentor. While the list is not exhaustive, some of the qualities of a good mentor are that he or she

1. offers acceptance and space to those who seek his or her assistance;
2. possesses an encouraging and contagious holiness;
3. exemplifies "extra-ordinariness," humility, transparency, and practicality;
4. offers perspective—especially in the darkness;
5. demonstrates the paradox of possibility and challenge;
6. is "un-self-conscious";
7. is able to be at home in the now;
8. does not seek answers as much as ways to live with the questions; and
9. does not get in the way of the message, remove the person's ultimate independence, or interfere with the movement of the Spirit.

In line with what is being looked for in the mentor, director, or guide, for our part, we must also seek to have or develop traits that complement the mentor's gifts. And so we must

1. be committed to act—not just desire or talk about change;
2. know why we are seeking a serious mentoring relationship;
3. appreciate what a contemporary *Abba* or *Amma* should truly be like when we are prepared to take the significant step to seek one or are asked to be such a presence for others;
4. be willing to be open to discovering new things about God, our faith, and ourselves—both our gifts and growing edges;
5. have a sense of the importance of developing a rule of prayer in line with what we learn from this relationship;
6. seek to "over-learn" the lessons learned so they will become part of our attitude and daily life rather than simply be compartmentalized into a so-called religious corner of our lives.

By having a mentor in the style described and a willingness to respectfully open ourselves to new dynamism in our faith, we will discover the path to the grace that is always there for us. And what a gift it is to us when the portals to greater inner freedom, love, and compassion show themselves because of this openness.

20.

Take a Different Route to Self-Knowledge: Intrigue

Self-knowledge is difficult under the best of circumstances. However, when we are feeling misunderstood, under stress, anxious, defensive, fearful, or unaccepted, then it is truly a journey without guide rails. Yet, when we are willing to recognize how much our own thoughts and beliefs are responsible for the problems we are experiencing, to withdraw the projections of our problems onto other people, and to stop demanding results on our time schedule, possibilities where there were seemingly none will present themselves.

And so self-knowledge must first come by seeding a sense of what I call "intrigue" within us. Intrigue is a posture of leaning back from emotions and nonjudgmentally looking at what we and others have done. These actions may have been in response to or to initiate something, and they may have either minimized or exacerbated a problem. In any case, we focus on how and why we choose or hold on to unsatisfying circumstances and relationships, without criticizing or blaming either ourselves or others. We can do that most effectively by focusing on the specific events to see how we can improve our relationship with ourselves and others.

Planning, creativity, and a willingness—maybe even the courage—to take action help us not only to learn about ourselves but also to try out what we have learned and see how it needs to be modified. The route of intrigue is truly a different road for us to take because of the conditioning of the world. Society traditionally says—and political pundits will model this well—that it needs to be somebody's fault. We need to blame ourselves or others. Yet, this generally leads us nowhere.

Yet, if we look as objectively as possible at life, we can see where we play a role for better or worse. This insight should not be a source of self-blame but an approach that allows us to retrieve the power we have given away. Even under awful situations, this is necessary.

I remember a colleague years ago who felt abandoned at work and home. In response, she had the humility and commonsense to go into therapy for support and clarification. She knew that continuing to live that way was not only unbearable but, because of her knowledge as a psychologist, to a great extent unnecessary. When she told me about it, I applauded her for her decision. "It is a good time to treat yourself to some time for reflection and feedback." However, knowing that danger always accompanies opportunity, I added, "There is a danger, though, which as a therapist you of course know as you enter this process."

When she asked me what danger I perceived, I went on, "Well, you are now feeling very put-upon and misunderstood. And so it would be understandable for you to go into therapy with the hope that one of the kind, reinforcing things that would happen would be that the therapist would agree with your perceptions of the situation. However, the therapist can only be on your side when she is on the side of seeing things as clearly as possible—not as a source of blame for you or others but so that you can understand as well as possible what *you* can do to make things better. Although we are psychologists, we well know that no matter how much the situation may be caused by people and events in the environment, it is our perception of them that matters. The real power over how life turns out is within our hands, not others'."

Spiritual wisdom is about seeing clearly, being gentle in how we approach ourselves and others, and not letting our opinions and habits block the Spirit of God from working within us. Without intrigue, not only is psychological maturity held back, but so is the search for God that is at the heart of inner formation. Essentially, such intrigue is at the heart of my writing this book, if I may say so, for persons such as yourself who are reading it.

If we are going to go through the doorways that God has opened for us, we must have that sense of intrigue. If we are going to respond to Jesus' central call to be compassionate, we must keep a sense of intrigue in our heart. When we do this, we will be able to focus on faithfulness like never before. We will become like archers: success won't be a distraction, and the arrow will flow freely toward its mark. This intrigue has been the goal of these twenty lessons and remains the objective of the next two parts in this book.

Part II

The Call and Three Doorways

Where the Twenty Lessons
Are Leading Us

Christianity is a community religion: we go toward or away from God *together*. For this to happen well, as we know, each of us must take our own spiritual lives seriously—not just with words said or out of guilt, duty, or fear, but with actions that come from an attitude of gratitude and compassion. Such an attitude makes life good for us and others because our lives are inextricably intertwined. But to accomplish this, we must attend to our own personal formation in order to follow the call given to us in the parable of the Good Samaritan to "go and do likewise." Let's take a moment to reread it here:

There was a scholar of the law who stood up to test him and said, "Teacher, what must I do to inherit eternal life?"

Jesus said to him, "What is written in the law? How do you read it?"

He said in reply,
You shall love the Lord, your God,
with all your heart,
with all your being,
with all your strength,
and with all your mind,
and your neighbor as yourself.

He replied to him, "You have answered correctly; do this and you will live."

But because he wished to justify himself, he said to Jesus, "And who is my neighbor?"

Jesus replied, "A man fell victim to robbers as he went down from Jerusalem to Jericho. They stripped and beat him and went off leaving him half-dead. A priest happened to be going down that road, but when he saw him, he passed by on the opposite side. Likewise a Levite came to the place, and when he saw him, he passed by on the opposite side.

"But a Samaritan traveler who came upon him was moved with compassion at the sight. He approached the victim, poured oil and wine over his wounds and bandaged them. Then he lifted him up on his own animal, took him to an inn, and cared for him.

"The next day he took out two silver coins and gave them to the innkeeper with the instruction, 'Take care of him. If you spend more than what I have given you, I shall repay you on my way back.'

"Which of these three, in your opinion, was the neighbor to the robbers' victim?" He answered, "The one who treated him with mercy." Jesus said to him, "Go and do likewise."

To follow this call from Jesus is to meet the greatest challenge in life and, in the process, to find ourselves and God more deeply. Yet, in today's stressful world it can be very dangerous.

Recently I was asked to speak in Germany to United States Army chaplains. As I was getting ready to walk up to give my first presentation, a seasoned chaplain and colonel walked over to me. He gently put his hand on my arm and said, "Many of the persons in this room are ghosts inside. After all they have seen and done to help others in Afghanistan and Iraq, there is nothing left."

I have heard this comment in different forms as I have traveled around the world working with "Good Samaritans"—priests, nuns, ministers, Christian lay leaders, physicians, nurses, psychologists, counselors, educators, relief and social workers, as well as others in the helping and healing professions. Yet, despite the odds that people face today—be they professionals or those who are simply trying to raise a family, support a parent, or be a good spouse, friend, or co-worker—I have hope that they can regain perspective when it is lost, remain a good Samaritan for others, and in the process find themselves and God in new ways. The reason behind this hope is rooted in a memorable encounter.

There are times in life when an interaction has the power to change us radically *if* we are graced enough to embrace it. One such dramatic interaction for me took place through sacred scripture when, as a young adult, I read the lead-in passage to the parable of the Good Samaritan (Lk 10:25–27). As a result, for the past thirty years I have based both my life and work on it. And as time has gone on, I believe more and more that this passage is the gateway to a full life—not just for me but for anyone who is truly open to the depth of its meaning and who is willing to put one's identity on the line in reading and absorbing its personal import. As theologian Karl Barth once indicated, when we read scripture and ask, "What is this book saying?" the text will respond, "Who is it that is asking?" This brief passage from Luke relates the most essential question we can ask; offers the three spiritual doorways to living fully; and invites us to embrace a new countercultural way of responding to Jesus' call in a manner that emphasizes faithfulness, not success. We need only have the eyes to see for the parable of the Good Samaritan to take root. Yet, for this to occur we need to embark on a lifelong pilgrimage to embrace the forgotten cardinal virtue of the desert: humility.

The Question and Three Doorways

Once again (because it is essential for personal formation and what we have done in this book), the passage that leads into the parable of the Good Samaritan begins with a classic rabbinical question for Jesus. It was asked of all teachers of the day (as it still should be asked today in some form or other): "Teacher what must I do to inherit eternal life?" As is common for Jesus, he in turn responds, "What is written in the law?" He also adds a second question to call the scholar deeper: "How do you read it?" to which the scholar answers:

You shall love the Lord, your God,
with all your heart,
with all your being,
with all your strength,
and with all your mind,
and your neighbor as yourself.

Jesus then responds, "You have answered correctly; *do this and you will live.*"

If this statement by the Lord is not powerful enough for us to see that he is providing special insight into the three doorways to the spiritual life—and all of life, really—we must remember that this passage echoes what was written earlier in Matthew's gospel (22:34–40). In this passage, it is Jesus this time who is asked by the Pharisees, "Teacher, which commandment in the law is the greatest?" He then does what rabbis in general often do: he first puts those listening to him at ease and then pulls out the rug from under them so they may see the passages and themselves anew. He did this, of course, by reaching into the Torah. But how he selects from scripture—in this case Leviticus and Deuteronomy—changes life for the people listening and for us.

First, he puts the crowd at ease by selecting a heavy precept and holding it before them: "You must love the Lord your God with all your heart, and with all your soul, and with all your mind. This is the greatest and first commandment." One can practically see the heads nodding in agreement—after all, how can someone disagree with this statement of faith? Then while they are at ease with what he said first, he shocks them by selecting a light precept and holding it up on the same level as the heavier one, "And a second is like it: 'You shall love your neighbor as yourself.'"

In emphasizing the neighbor, Jesus is reinforcing the law given by God to Moses during the Exodus. Jesus asks his listeners to see anew that love expressed through vertical prayer to God is intimately connected to horizontal love shown to one's neighbor. But he also uses what we would now see as a circular, feminine image when he says, "And you shall love your neighbor *as yourself.*" In doing this, he is indicating quite simply that one of the greatest gifts a person can share with others is a sense of one's own peace and perspective—but you can't share what you don't have!

And so, in both Matthew and Luke, we are given three doorways to a rich spiritual and psychological life: namely, *presence to others; presence to self* through self-care, self-love, and self-understanding; and the ultimate doorway, *presence to God.*

The Call . . . Go and Do Likewise

The doorways and the call are both before us. They are in plain sight—clear and compelling. However, when we seek to respond, the water gets murky for even the holiest, most committed, and most talented among us. As a matter of fact, our response to this call—both consciously and unconsciously—will take our entire lifetimes. We must continue to fathom the meaning of this call at each stage of our lives. Given this reality, this book will address personal formation with three questions that correspond to the three doorways that Jesus offers us. Each day, we have a choice to respond to, ignore, or evade these questions.

• How can I more completely love my "neighbor" in the broadest, deepest sense of that term?
• Can I love myself in good ways so I can meet Jesus' call to "go and do likewise?"
• And finally and most crucially, how can I more fully love God?

These are certainly the three most serious questions of life that we must consider as we go forth. How we understand them, and how we grapple and balance our responses to them, can well determine whether we will burn out or burn up with the Spirit in life.

The First Doorway: Love of Neighbor

Many years ago, I led a week-long retreat near what was once known as the Gulf of Siam. The attendees were priests, nuns, and lay missioners who had come from Nepal, Vietnam, Thailand, and Bangladesh.

After one of the sessions on compassion that was roughly based on the parable of the Good Samaritan, I asked if there were any questions. In response, one of the participants, a gentle, seasoned priest whose mission was in Bangladesh, raised his hand and asked, "How many bodies can I step over before I stop to pick one up?" As a quiet hush settled over for the group, I paused until he had a chance to amplify his remark before I tried to respond. He went on, "You see, there are so many needs that I don't know where to begin or how I could possibly manage many, much less all, of what I am confronted with in my ministry among the dire poor of the country where I serve."

Although many of us may not be faced with such dramatic poverty, sickness, and death each day, the questions still remain for us: "How can we extend our emotional flame to others without being burned out in the process? Which crosses am I being called to carry, and which am I not?"

But these questions, though worthy of being addressed in this section, are not sufficient if we only seek answers to them. While we must respond to them, there are other questions that must also be addressed: "How can we, as Good Samaritans, be faithful in a manner that will help us see God in new ways? How can reaching out be part of a circle of grace in which we can be called to *both* deeper compassion and inner fulfillment? How we address these questions will be crucial to whether or not we live life as fully as possible.

The Second Doorway: Love Yourself

If we are truly to fight the good fight, we must learn early on that being compassionate to others doesn't mean ignoring ourselves. As a matter of fact, the long road of true friendship relies on having a good relationship with ourselves. As Pope John XXIII once said, "Whoever has a heart full of love always has something to share." This wisdom is recognized in many cultures. The Ibo of Nigeria have a saying, "It is the heart that gives . . . the fingers just let go."

Just as it is erroneous to think that you can love God while not loving others around you, it is ludicrous to think that loving God or others can be done while despising or not caring for yourself. Moreover, being grateful for all the gifts you have been given and enjoying them is one of the most beautiful prayers you can make to God. Think back to the beginning of this book and the story of a little girl who is given a Christmas gift. What is the nicest thank-you to receive for such a gesture? Why, of course, it is to see her both enjoy the gift and freely share it with others. The same can be said of our lives.

And so, utilizing the same information shared with professional helpers and healers to help them love, take care of, and know themselves in order to continue their ministry, this second doorway will offer simple, effective guidance on how to remain vital and alive in the most difficult and draining of situations. Remember: it is not the amount of darkness in the world, our work, our family, or even in ourselves that matters. It is how we stand in that darkness that makes the difference.

Knowing this and how to remain alive and vital can allow us to see Jesus' call to "go and do likewise" in a radically different way. Rather than concerning ourselves with success or failure, guilt or duty, we can reach out in a spirit of personal faithfulness that not only will serve to help others but will change us for the better in the process as well.

The Third Doorway: "You Must Love God with Your Whole Heart . . ."

The renowned spiritual writer Henri Nouwen had the good fortune to have as a spiritual guide the Trappist monk, abbot, and psychiatrist John Eudes Bamberger. At one of their spiritual-direction sessions during Henri's nine-month stay at the abbey, which lead to the publication of *The Genesee Diary*, Henri shared what he felt might be a too basic and possibly naïve question, "When I pray, to whom do I pray?" "When I say 'Lord,' what do I mean?"

He was surprised when John Eudes responded very differently than he expected. He said, "This is the real question, this is the most important question you can raise; at least this is the question you can make your most important question. . . . You will discover that it involves every part of yourself because the question, 'Who is the Lord to whom I pray?' leads directly to the question, 'Who am I who wants to pray to the Lord?' And then you will soon wonder, 'Why is the Lord of Justice also the Lord of Compassion?' This leads you to the center of meditation."

John Eudes then pointed out that facing the original question about to whom you are praying "requires a certain decision to make that question the center of your meditation. If you do so, you will realize that you are embarking on a long road, a very long road."

To take this journey, each of us—as in the early Church—must develop our own rule of prayer. And so the call to "go and do likewise" with respect to reaching out to others is not simply an impossible request to add to all that already faces us in a troubled world. When our response is based on both a healthy love of self and a deep love of God, it is a call to go through the three doorways that will lead us to a place where we can experience life as never before. That is what this book has addressed as both you and I seek to simultaneously receive and share friendship—*especially* with God—in ways we have possibly not experienced before.

Part III

Developing Your Own
Inner Workshop of Virtue

A Month of Simple Questions
and Exercises

Now it is your turn: take a few moments to reflect on the lessons being offered so you can put them into practice in your own way, in your unique situation. The following practices and questions may represent a challenge to habitual ways of thinking, perceiving, and understanding.

Our journey through life becomes truly spiritual and full when it plumbs the depth of the way we are now thinking about ourselves, others, the world, and God. Working with the following exercises and questions is a commitment to make life more of what it can be—a fuller experience of God's gift of life to us all. Even in seemingly insignificant moments, life can open up. When we begin to hear the light rustle of the leaves instead of our own preoccupations during an early morning or evening walk, we realize we are becoming aware of the whispers of God now, right here in our daily life.

Phil Cousineau relates an interaction in his book *The Art of Pilgrimage* that demonstrates how different life can be when we are willing to risk encountering the sacred. In his case it was a new friend who encouraged him to do so. While he speaks about transforming travel, I think his words also address how we can traverse our lives each day:

Ahmet's respectful tone of voice sounded like a blessing. By naming my journey a pilgrimage, he had conferred a kind of dignity on it that altered the way I have traveled ever since. . . . In the more than twenty years since that journey, I've traveled around the world, marveling both at its seven-times-seven thousand wonders, and at the frustration of fellow travelers I saw at the same sites, whose faces, if not their voices, cried out like the torch singer, *"Is that all there is?"* . . . If we truly want to know the secret of soulful travel, we need to believe that there is something sacred waiting to be discovered in virtually every journey. . . . Always it is a journey of risk and renewal. For a journey without challenge has no meaning; one without purpose has no goal.

And so take a few minutes each day over the next month to read the question or exercise proposed, reflect on each of them, and write your response. Then finally put into action in some way what you believe will enable you to transform your day and the rest of your life into a true pilgrimage toward greater self-understanding and expression, toward compassion, and toward God. If it feels a bit much, remember once again that the philosophy at hand is to *just start where you are.*

Day One

Uncovering Your Gifts

Make a list of all the gifts and talents God has given the world through your presence in it. If you have a hard time developing this list, ask others who know you to give you their impressions of what they are. It is important that this list be as extensive as possible because you need to be aware of what gifts or charisms you have been given to share with others. Otherwise, the people around you might lose the benefits God intended to offer them through you.

Day Two

Enhancing, Enjoying, and Sharing Your Gifts

In what ways have you sought to take care of the very gifts and talents God has given to you? What are some illustrations of ways you have shared these gifts with different types of people in varied circumstances?

Day Three

Pruning Your Gifts

Under what circumstances do your gifts actually turn out to be a liability—not because of the resistance of others, but because of your own insecurities, your desire to build up your own ego, or for some other defensive reason?

Day Four

Savoring Life

What are some of the little ways you savor the daily gifts of life? When you reflect on this question, include family, friends, coworkers, and people you meet by chance along with the objects and opportunities of life.

Day Five

Seeing the Shy Stag

Both spiritually and psychologically, humility is like a shy stag. What are some ways that you catch yourself over- or underestimating your gifts or boosting your ego to impress others in some way? (Remember: underestimating yourself is not humility. Humility helps us to see ourselves realistically so we don't waste energy building ourselves up or hiding our gifts so that no one can benefit from them.)

Day Six

Getting Out of Yourself

Novelist Henry James reportedly uttered the admonishment: "Get out of yourself and stay out!" How do you know when you are overinvolved in yourself and your troubles? What are the signals for you that you have spent enough time fully exploring your own feelings and hurts and how they have impacted you, so you know to look outward toward the feelings and needs of others?

Day Seven

The Threefold Call

What comes to mind when you hear the threefold call?

Love God deeply; do what you can for others; and, please, take good care of yourself.

Day Eight

Wonder and Awe

In entering the doorways to awe in your own life, what are some of the simple ways you might experience the luminescence in the ordinary? In other words, in addition to the major events that have taken your breath away and possibly have been transformative epiphanies, what are the little encounters with God's wonders that you relish?

Day Nine

Pacing Your Life, Seeing the Signposts

Reflect on the ways you slow down to notice the signposts that God has put in your life. What are some of these signposts, both past and present? What are additional ways you can notice them? For instance, is it possible to see a disruption as a grace, or an unexpected meeting in the hallway as an opportunity for compassion?

Day Ten

Responding, Not Reacting, to God

What are some of the ways that you review your day so you can learn from it in order to deepen, or perhaps alter, the way you become more responsive to God?

Day Eleven

Deep Gratefulness

How do you think you can be more grateful in life? (Please be specific.) Who or what would you miss most if you were to lose him, her, or it? Who or what can you not conceive of living without? Given that, in what ways do you show gratitude to the person and God for these persons, situations, or things?

Day Twelve

Relaxing Your Grasp

Provide some examples of ways that you can relax your grasp on life so you can enjoy everyone and everything that comes your way instead of being possessed by them.

Day Thirteen

Helping Sadness Become Spiritual Wisdom

When you become sad, negative, or discouraged during the day because of something that has happened, what are some of the ways you can mine that sadness to learn from it and to find where you are vulnerable and what you are holding onto?

Day Fourteen

Past Gems of Sadness

What are some examples of times in the past when fleeting, unexpected experiences of sadness have helped you understand yourself and life better? How does this knowledge help you now?

Day Fifteen

Real Interest in Others

There once was a fellow who tended to go into a rage if you disagreed with him or encouraged him to look at himself when he did something that was unkind. He also could be very self-centered at times and even be a bit of a bully. Yet, he had many friends—me included. As I thought about why this was so, I realized that he had an amazing ability to demonstrate interest in what people were about. When he asked you how you were, he was truly interested and would even follow up with a call to see how what you described to him was developing. When we stop someone in the hallway and ask, "How are you doing?" do we really mean it? Are there ways you can become more mindful of others so they can experience real interest in them from another human being?

Day Sixteen

Realizing the Rituals

What are some of the rituals you undertake during the day and week that help you appreciate life and the presence of God within you more clearly? Some may be obvious, like morning prayer. Others may not be so plainly religious but still prayerful, like a quiet cup of tea in the afternoon while looking out the window. Be creative and reflective with this question as a way of expanding your recognition of the rituals you are now enjoying. And add new rituals to your repertoire!

Day Seventeen

Lean Back

Discovering what God is teaching you through your emotions is one of the most enlightening ways of self-exploration and self-understanding. With this in mind, the next time you experience anger, annoyance, or discouragement, *lean back* and reflect to see what you can learn about yourself. In this way, rather than reacting to others, you can create some distance from your emotions. Then your response can be more helpful and your understanding as to why this is touching you more clear.

Day Eighteen

Humor

List some times when you were able to relax and laugh at your own foibles. How did those events allow you to be light enough to better understand yourself and the current situation? Identify areas about which you are too sensitive and therefore unable to respond with humor or equanimity. What can the knowledge of this reality teach you about yourself?

Day Nineteen

A "Little Rule"

At this point, what do you include in your own "little rule" of prayer? Within that rule, what seems to be the most spiritually engaging for you? Are there other things you can add to your "little rule" that might enhance your sense of God in your life?

Day Twenty

The Limits of Life

Most people believe that the real limit in life is that we must die. Yet, length of life doesn't ensure that you appreciate your life more. However, those who are aware of the fact that they may die at any moment—as far-fetched as that might seem—are able to enjoy their life and be present to others more compassionately. And so reflect during the day that you are dying and that the person you are speaking to is dying as well. Come back to this reflection often during the day, and then on the drive or walk home or when getting ready for bed reflect back to see what impact this exercise has had on you.

Day Twenty-One

Self-Talk

During or after interchanges in the course of the day, be more aware of the self-talk that is going on in your head. Ask yourself why you are feeling positive, negative, or neutral about someone or some event. Don't assume you know the answer, and when you come up with an answer, push yourself and ask further questions: "Yes, but are there other reasons why I feel and think this way? When have I felt this way before?"

Day Twenty-Two

Savoring the Silence and Possibly the Solitude

Reflect on places where you have experienced a silence that was renewing or revealing to you in some way. Then ask yourself if there are places now where you can spend a minute or two, possibly a half hour, a day in silence and even solitude. Finally, determine how well you are using these places of quiet and how you can best assemble crumbs of alonetime in order to center yourself and simply breathe.

Day Twenty-Three

Practice Nonjudgmental Presence

For the rest of the day, seek simply to observe what is going on in others and yourself without judging. Don't look at the day and wish it were something else or be jubilant that it is sunny, but simply observe. When you become angry, look at yourself as if you were someone else. When someone behaves in a particular way, simply note the reaction, not the cause. To observe without the interference of our ego is very difficult, but it will provide a great deal of worthwhile information.

Day Twenty-Four

Mentor in the Mind

Decide who you find to be an ideal mentor—a living person, someone you have read about, or an historical figure. Once you have done that, list the gifts that attracted you to this person. Ask yourself what you hope to gain from being mentored by this person. Then seek to put into action the very traits that you are hoping to develop as a result of the interaction.

Day Twenty-Five

Change the Limited Reputation You Have with Yourself

What is the reputation you have with yourself? What and who do you think contributed to that story? Given the chance, your story could be much bigger if you could see yourself more as God sees you. How do you think God sees you? What actions can you take to break the habit of confining your views of yourself to those you have absorbed from others?

Day Twenty-Six

Take a Walk, Not a Think

Most people, when they go for a walk, really don't notice the terrain they are walking through or the breeze in the air. They are in a cognitive cocoon, thinking about some event, interaction, need, or achievement. Mindful walking is both prayerful and renewing. It involves being centered on a word or a feeling and bringing yourself back to that as you walk and look and listen without judgment to what is around you. Seeing, not labeling, and enjoying, not taking a mental picture, is part of being alive. Doing it more can have a major impact on your total life. Seek to take a mindful walk today.

Day Twenty-Seven

Standing on an Obstacle

The sense we get from religious figures is that spiritual depth doesn't come from going around obstacles we encounter in life but in utilizing them in the right way to learn and become deeper. The Dalai Lama, who has been through so much with the takeover of his country and the killing and imprisonment of so many of his people, believes that if you utilize obstacles properly, they result in greater courage, intelligence, and wisdom. On the other hand, if you don't, then discouragement, a sense of failure, and even depression might result. Given this theme, reflect now on the obstacles you have encountered in your life. While they have been difficult for you, looking back, in what ways have they resulted in your becoming a more spiritually attuned person?

Day Twenty-Eight

Being a Peacemaker

Each of us is expected to be a peacemaker in some way. Given your personality and experience, how have you been a peacemaker in the past? In what ways can you be an even better peacemaker in the future?

Day Twenty-Nine

In the Presence of God

Robert Lax, minimalist poet and friend of the contemplative Thomas Merton, became interested in what it would be like to see oneself living always before God. He was encouraged in this direction through contact with an Eastern religious guide who trusted God in all things and sought to live his whole life that way. Spiritual guide and author Henri Nouwen, in his book *Clowning in Rome*, put it this way:

> To pray does not primarily mean to think about God in contrast to thinking about other things, or to spend time with God instead of spending time with other people. Rather it means to think and to live in the presence of God. As soon as we begin to divide our thoughts about God and thoughts about people and events, we remove God from our daily life and put him in a pious niche where we can think pious thoughts and experience pious feelings.

What would it be like for you to seek to live your life in the presence of God? How are you already putting your trust in God, and what are the areas that still need to be placed in God's hands?

Day Thirty

Motives: Ours and God's

In his book *Gifts of the Desert*, Kyriacos Markides describes his visits to Mount Athos, a very holy place in Christianity. In relating his experiences, he notes that one of the elders there told him, "A person may have his reasons for visiting Mount Athos, but God may have his." In the case of this book, you have had your own reasons for picking it up and reading it. What are those reasons? Now consider why God might have wanted you to read it.

Conclusion:
A Few Final Words of Encouragement

Eugene H. Peterson, in his book *Christ Plays in Ten Thousand Places*, writes, "Without wonder we approach life as a self-help project. We employ techniques; we analyze gifts and potentialities; we set goals and assess progress. Spiritual formation is reduced to cosmetics." Instead, formation is about living who you are more fully by seeking in every way possible to place yourself in the presence of a God who is calling you to be all you can be by enjoying your gifts and sharing them freely. That is what this book seeks to help you do.

For this, as Terry Hershey notes in the following story from his delightful work *The Power of Pause*, we need conducive space:

> Every day after school, the son of a well-known rabbi would enter his house, place his backpack on the dining room table, leave the house through the back door, and head into the woods behind the house.
>
> At first, the rabbi gave little thought to his son's ritual. But it continued for days, and then for weeks. Every day, out into the woods for almost half an hour. The rabbi grew concerned.
>
> "My son," he said one day. "I notice that every day you leave our home to spend time in the woods. What is it you are doing there?"

"Oh, Papa," the son replied. "There is no need to worry. I go into the woods to pray. It is in the woods that I can talk to God."

"Oh," the rabbi said, clearly relieved. "But, as the son of a rabbi, you should know that God is the same everywhere."

"Yes, Papa. I know that God is the same everywhere. But, I am not."

Once we find the space we need to pray and grow, we then can see that what happens in prayer can positively affect the rest of our lives. As a matter of fact, if it doesn't, then the space and prayer are of questionable value.

The ramifications of our contemplative experiences with God take deeper root in our lives through the rituals and activities of our "little rules" of prayer. But more than that, these transformative moments, which take place when we step through the doorway to a deep encounter with the divine, should affect how we live with others and, most importantly, with ourselves.

Prayerful mindfulness should allow us to begin to balance gentleness with clarity, to view ourselves nonjudgmentally, and to learn with a spirit of intrigue about our gifts and growing edges. We find that life then becomes, not a series of successes or failures, but adventures in learning and living. We watch ourselves less and live more naturally, and because of this others can more easily do the same. They can see we are not asking them to believe in *us* in order for this to happen. Rather, they observe that we believe in *them*, and that makes all the difference.

In 1945 an explorer from Los Angeles named John G. Bourne traveled through eastern Chiapas in Mexico. What he saw changed him dramatically. When he returned to Mexico again in 1946 with another explorer, Herman Charles Frey, they became the first non-Mayans to see the ruins of Bonampak, touted as the Sistine Chapel of the ancient Mayan civilization. This encounter led to a life of deep interest in this civilization, as well as a gathering of its artifacts so the world could appreciate a little of what he had experienced.

The same type of experience is waiting for us as we seek to allow Christ to "make all things new" in our lives. When we open ourselves up through a more intentional life of ongoing formation and prayer, we will reap great benefits for ourselves and others. Comparing spiritual formation with the adventures of John Bourne may seem odd. Yet, I mean it to be a call to you to begin or continue your inner workshop instead of settling for so much less. Just start where you are now. God will do the rest.

Be well . . .
Robert J. Wicks

References

A Brief Introduction: Create an Inner Workshop
France, Peter. *Patmos.* New York: Atlantic Monthly Press, 2002.
Kornfield, Jack. *After the Ecstasy, the Laundry.* New York: Bantam, 2000.

1. Live (Don't Only Say) a Simple Prayer
Ellsberg, Robert. *The Saints' Guide to Happiness.* New York: North Point Press, 2003.

4. Appreciate the Strength of Inner Simplicity
Ricard, Matthieu. *Happiness.* Boston: Little, Brown, 2006.

5. When Invited, Enter the Doorway to Awe
Heschel, Abraham Joshua. *I Asked for Wonder.* Edited by Samuel Dresner. New York: Crossroad, 1983.
Coehlo, Paulo. *The Alchemist.* New York: HarperCollins, 2006.

7. Avoid "Spiritual Alzheimer's"
Steindl-Rast, David. *Gratefulness, the Heart of Prayer: An Approach to Life in Fullness.* Mahwah, NJ: Paulist Press, 1990.

8. Honor the Spirituality of Letting Go
Chadwick, David. *The Crooked Cucumber.* New York: Broadway, 1999.
de Mello, Anthony. *The Way to Love.* New York: Image, 2012
Simmons, Philip. *Learning to Fall.* New York: Bantam, 2002.

9. Mine the Wisdom of Spiritual Sadness
Housden, Roger. *Ten Poems to Change Your Life.* New York: Harmony, 2001.

10. Adjust Your Inner Lens
Kornfield, Jack. *After the Ecstasy, the Laundry.* New York: Bantam, 2000.

11. Discover Both Your Gifts and Growing Edges
Seligman, Martin. *Authentic Happiness: Using the New Positive Psychology to Realize Your Potential for Lasting Fulfillment.* New York: Free Press, 2002.

13. Welcome the Softening Place of Humor
Mott, Michael. *The Seven Mountains of Thomas Merton.* Boston: Houghton-Mifflin, 1984.
Rowland, Penelope. *Paris Was Ours.* New York: Algonquin Books, 2011.

14. Establish a "Little Rule" of Your Own
Kornfield, Jack. *After the Ecstasy, the Laundry.* New York: Bantam, 2000.

15. Understand the Important Role of Death . . . While You're Still Alive!
De Montaigne, Michel. *Selected Essays.* Cambridge, MA: Hackett, 2012.
Bode, Richard. *First You Have to Row a Little Boat.* New York: Warner, 1993.

16. Be More Attuned to the Power of Your Attitude and Self-Talk
Moorehead, Caroline. *Gellhorn: A Twentieth-Century Life.* New York: Holt, 2004.
Kornfield, Jack. *After the Ecstasy, the Laundry.* New York: Bantam, 2000.
Wicks, Robert. *Seeds of Sensitivity.* Notre Dame, Indiana: Ave Maria Press, 1995.

18. Savor Some Silence Each Day
Grumbach, Doris. *Fifty Days of Solitude.* Boston: Beacon Press, 1994.

19. Emulate the Right Persons to Follow the Path of Grace
Harford, James. *Merton and Friends.* New York: Continuum, 2006.
Wicks, Robert. *Crossing the Desert.* Notre Dame, Indiana: Sorin Books, 2007.

Part II: The Call and Three Doorways
Nouwen, Henri J. M. *The Genesee Diary.* New York: Image, 1981.

Part III: Developing Your Own Inner Workshop of Virtue
Cousineau, Phil. *The Art of Pilgrimage.* Berkeley: Conari Press, 1998.

Day Twenty-Nine
Nouwen, Henri J. M. *Clowning in Rome.* New York: Image, 1979.

Day Thirty
Markides, Kyriacos. *Gifts of the Desert.* New York: Doubleday, 2005.

Conclusion: A Few Final Words of Encouragement
Peterson, Eugene H. *Christ Plays in Ten Thousand Places.* Grand Rapids, MI: Wm. B. Eerdmans, 2005.
Hershey, Terry. *The Power of Pause.* Chicago: Loyola Press, 2009.

Robert J. Wicks, who received his doctorate in psychology from Hahnemann Medical College, is on the faculty of Loyola University Maryland. Wicks has taught in universities and professional schools of psychology, medicine, social work, nursing, and theology. He was responsible for the psychological debriefing of relief workers following the Rwandan genocide and also worked with relief teams in Cambodia. Additionally, he delivered presentations at Walter Reed Army Hospital to health care professionals involved in caring for Iraqi war veterans with amputations and severe head injuries. He has authored more than fifty books, including *Streams of Contentment* and *Riding the Dragon*.